BEARPORT BIOGRAPHIES

MICHAEL JORDAN

BASKETBALL SUPERSTAR

by Rachel Rose

Consultant: Mike Chamberlain, Physical Educator

BEARPORT PUBLISHING

Minneapolis, Minnesota

Credits

Cover and title page, © landmarkmedia/Shutterstock; 4, © Reed Saxon/AP Images; 5, © Bob Galbraith/AP Images; 6, © Danita Delimont/Alamy Stock Photo; 8, © Raleigh News & Observer/TNS/Alamy Stock Photo; 9, © PCN Photography/Alamy Stock Photo; 10, © ZUMA Press Inc/Alamy Stock Photo; 11, © Kirthmon Dozier/AP Images; 12, © John McDonough/Icon SMI/Newscom; 13, © TNS/Newscom; 14, © Rob Tringali/SportsChrome/Newscom; 15, © Charles Cherney/KRT/Newscom; 16, © Collection Christophel/Alamy Stock Photo; 17, © KRT/Newscom; 18, © Chris Keane/Icon SMI/Newscom; 19, © Image of Sport/Newscom; 20, © MCT/Newscom; 21, © PCN Photography/Alamy Stock Photo; 22L, © KRT/Newscom; 22R, © Charles Cherney/KRT/Newscom; 22B, © MCT/Newscom

President: Jen Jenson
Director of Product Development: Spencer Brinker
Editor: Allison Juda

Library of Congress Cataloging-in-Publication Data

Names: Rose, Rachel, 1968- author.
Title: Michael Jordan : basketball superstar / by Rachel Rose.
Description: Minneapolis, Minnesota : Bearport Publishing Company, [2021] | Series: Bearport biographies | Includes bibliographical references and index.
Identifiers: LCCN 2020039235 (print) | LCCN 2020039236 (ebook) | ISBN 9781647477189 (library binding) | ISBN 9781647477264 (paperback) | ISBN 9781647477349 (ebook)
Subjects: LCSH: Jordan, Michael, 1963---Juvenile literature. | Basketball players--United States--Biography--Juvenile literature. | African American basketball players--Biography--Juvenile literature.
Classification: LCC GV884.J67 R65 2021 (print) | LCC GV884.J67 (ebook) | DDC 796.323092/2 [B]--dc23
LC record available at https://lccn.loc.gov/2020039235
LC ebook record available at https://lccn.loc.gov/2020039236

For more information, write to Bearport Publishing, 5357 Penn Avenue South, Minneapolis, MN 55419.
Printed in the United States of America.

Contents

Champion **4**

A Strong Start **6**

Career Highs **10**

I'm Back **14**

All-Time Great **20**

Timeline 22

Glossary 23

Index 24

Read More 24

Learn More Online 24

About the Author 24

Champion

Tears ran down Michael Jordan's face as he hugged the **trophy** close to him. He didn't know it then, but it would be the first of many times he would be holding the **championship** trophy. Michael had just led the Chicago Bulls to their game five win over the LA Lakers in the 1991 NBA Finals. Michael was also named the most valuable player (MVP).

Following the 1991 **victory**, Michael led the Bulls to two more championships in the next two seasons.

Michael during the 1991 NBA Finals

A Strong Start

Michael Jeffrey Jordan was born on February 17, 1963, in Brooklyn, New York. But he grew up in Wilmington, North Carolina. From an early age, he was a good athlete. Michael played baseball, basketball, and football. In high school, he **focused** on basketball. He was so good that he got a basketball **scholarship** to the University of North Carolina.

Michael didn't make the cut his first year trying out for his high school basketball team.

Michael quickly became a star player for the University of North Carolina Tar Heels. As a freshman, he made the winning shot in the 1982 college championship game against the Georgetown Hoyas. Soon, people began to take notice of the young athlete. In 1984, the Chicago Bulls picked him to play on their team.

Michael announced he would skip his senior year of college to join the Bulls.

Michael playing for the University of North Carolina

During his time as a Tar Heel, Michael was named College Player of the Year twice.

Career Highs

It wasn't long before Michael was making his mark in **professional** basketball. During his first season in the National Basketball Association (NBA), he was named **Rookie** of the Year. Michael also earned the nickname Air Jordan because of how high he could jump in the air while shooting. In 1984, he started teaming up with Nike to create Air Jordan sneakers.

Jordans quickly became some of the most popular sneakers around.

Michael is a star shooter. In 1987, he won the All-Star Slam Dunk contest.

Michael quickly rose to fame. In May 1989, he took what became known as "the shot" to win the nail-biting game against the Cleveland Cavaliers. In March 1990, Michael scored a whopping 69 points in another game against the Cavaliers. Later that year, he went on to win the first of his six NBA championships and the first of his five MVP titles.

Michael celebrates after making "the shot"

In 1992, Michael played on the Dream Team at the Olympic Games. They took home gold.

I'm Back

Tragedy struck Michael's family in 1993. His father was killed in a robbery, and Michael took the death very hard. He **retired** from basketball and turned to professional baseball. But after two years, he was ready to return to basketball. In 1995, he sent out the message, "I'm back." He was indeed back. Michael and the Bulls won the NBA Finals that year.

One of the reasons Michael played baseball was to honor his father, who had loved the game.

Michael proved he was back during the 1996 NBA Finals.

Michael played his last game for the Chicago Bulls on June 14, 1998. With just seconds left in the game against the Utah Jazz, the Bulls were down by one point. In true Michael Jordan style, he landed the game-winning shot, bringing the Bulls to their second **three-peat**.

Michael became a star both on and off the court. In 1996, he played himself in the movie *Space Jam*.

Michael brings the Bulls another victory during the 1998 NBA Finals.

In 1999, Michael retired again, but he returned to the game in 2001. This time, he played for the Washington Wizards. Two years later, Michael retired from playing basketball for good. But he didn't go far. Soon, Michael was working behind the scenes. He is currently the main owner of the Charlotte Hornets.

Michael first became an owner of the Charlotte basketball team in 2006. At that time, they were called the Bobcats.

Michael as a Wizard

All-Time Great

Michael Jordan was one of the greatest basketball players of all time. He had a lot of talent, but he also worked very hard. Michael is the first one to point out that he missed over 9,000 shots in his career and lost almost 300 games. But he knows that he had to fail at times in order to become a basketball superstar.

In 2009, Michael Jordan joined the Basketball Hall of Fame.

Michael holds a special place in history.

Timeline

Here are some key dates in Michael Jordan's life.

1963
Born on February 17

1985
Named NBA Rookie of the Year

1991
Wins first NBA Finals

1995
Returns to the Bulls after first retirement

1998
Completes second three-peat

2003
Retires for the final time

2009
Enters the Basketball Hall of Fame

2020
Stars in a documentary series called *The Last Dance*

Glossary

championship a contest or final game of a series that decides which team will be the winner

focused concentrated on one thing

professional paid to play a sport

retired gave up a job; stopped working

rookie a player who is in their first year

scholarship money given to a person to pay for school

three-peat three consecutive championships in sports

tragedy a terrible event that causes great sadness or suffering

trophy a prize

victory the act of defeating another team

Index

baseball 6, 14
Basketball Hall of Fame 20, 22
Charlotte Hornets 18
Chicago Bulls 4, 8, 14, 16–17, 22
high school 6–7
MVP 4, 12
NBA Finals 4–5, 14–15, 17, 22
retirement 14, 18, 22
rookie 10, 22
Space Jam 16
University of North Carolina Tar Heels 6, 8–9
Washington Wizards 18–19

Read More

Levit, Joe. *Michael Jordan: Flying High (Epic Sports Bios)*. Minneapolis: Lerner Publications, 2021.

Mason, Tyler. *Michael Jordan and the Chicago Bulls (Sports Dynasties)*. Minneapolis: Abdo Publishing, 2019.

Learn More Online

1. Go to **www.factsurfer.com**
2. Enter "**Michael Jordan**" into the search box.
3. Click on the cover of this book to see a list of websites.

About the Author

Rachel Rose is a writer who lives in San Francisco. Her favorite books to write are about people who lead inspiring lives.